At Least I'm Getting Better!

poems for kids and other people

Written by Judy Lalli

Photographs by Douglas L. Mason-Fry

Third Printing, 1988

ISBN 0-935648-15-1

Contents

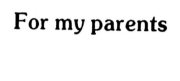
For my parents

CAN CHOOSE

I can choose
To win or lose.
It's all in how I see it.

If I think that
I'm a winner,
Pretty soon I'll be it.

Hands can fight.
Hands can scare.
Or
Hands can come together
And show they care.

THE SHOWS ARE GREAT

The shows are great,
The colors are bright.
I carry it with me day and night.

But I don't watch any TV station.
I just adjust my imagination.

HALLOWEEN DISGUISE

What should I be on Halloween?
A ghost?
A witch?
A king?
A queen?

I can't decide what I should be,
'Cause most of the time
I like being me.

NICKNAMES

Crybaby, crybaby,
Half-pint, dummy.
Nicknames make me feel so crummy.

Names can never hurt me,
But just the same,
Call me by my very own name.

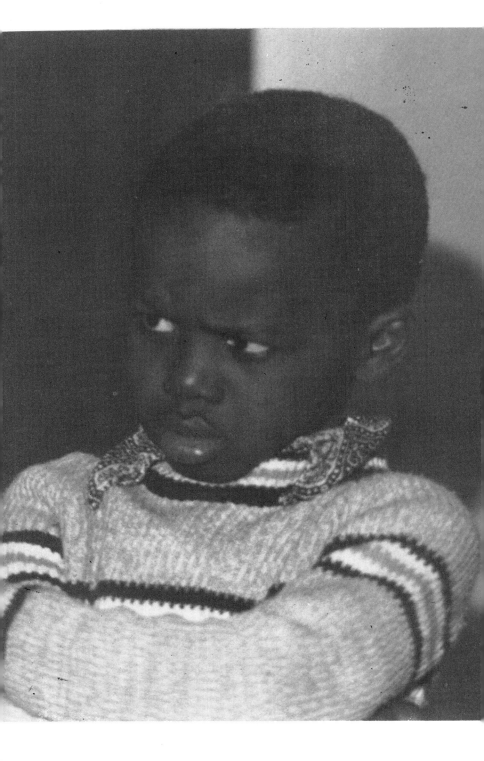

WHEN I'M CRANKY

When I'm cranky
I sass my mother,
I kick my toys,
I boss my brother.

I think what I should do instead,
Is
Jog
Or
Jump
Or
Go to bed.

I CAN'T MOVE IT

I can't move it,
You can't move it,
It won't move an inch.

But if we pull together,
Moving it's a cinch.

I DIDN'T BELIEVE I COULD DO IT

I didn't believe I could do it.
I was afraid to try.
My teacher said, "I always knew it."
And next time, so will I.

FIVE LITTLE PEOPLE

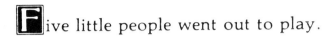ive little people went out to play.

The first one said,
"Do it my way."
The second one said,
"That's no fair."
The third one said,
"I don't care."
The fourth one said,
"Where's all the fun?"
The fifth one said,
"This game is done."

So five little people all walked away.
They never even got to play.

NEW STYLE

Here's an idea for a brand new style:
Everybody wear a great big SMILE.

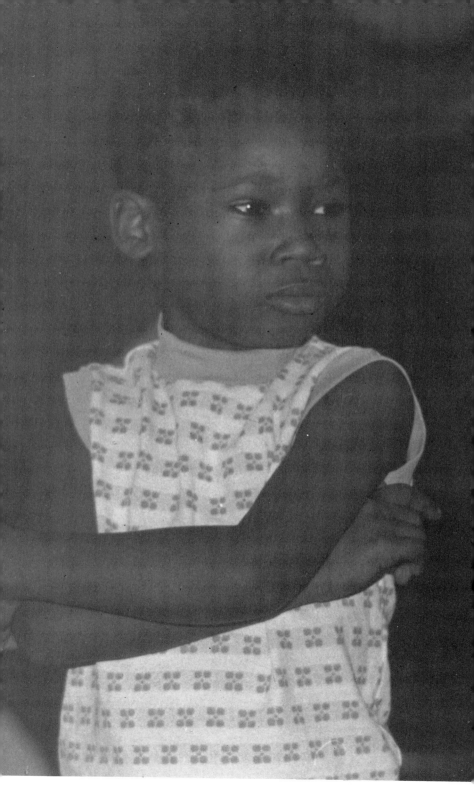

WISHES

Now I'm five.
I wish I were ten.
But then I'd wish I were five again.

Now I'm little.
I wish I were tall.
But then I'd wish that I were small.

Now I'm here.
I wish I were there.
But then I'd wish I were everywhere.

I'm tired of wishing.
I think I'll vow
To start being happy
Right here and now.

WE'RE O.K.

I like me and
I like you.
Together there's a lot that
We can do.

We're not the same
In every way,
But I'm O.K. and
You're O.K.

BROKEN WAGON

I'm mad.
It looks bad.
I think I broke my wagon.

The wheel is bent.
It has a dent.
And everything is draggin'.

Oh, what's the use?
The handle's loose.
I hope somebody kicks it.

I want to shout
And throw it out.

But I think I'd better fix it.

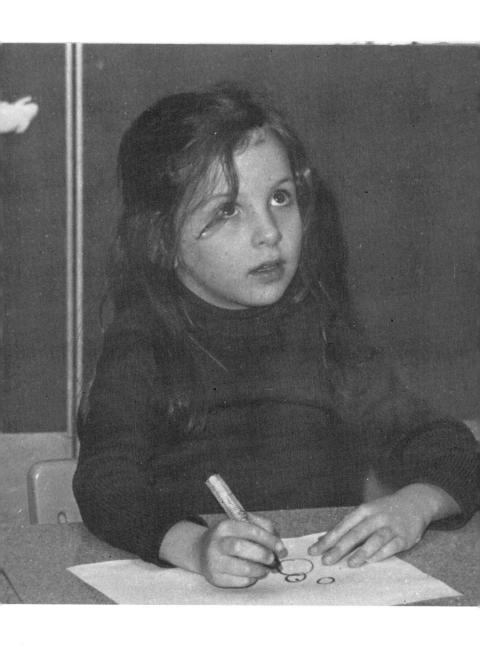

I'M A PERSON, TOO

You may be big,
I may be little,
But I'm a person, too.

So treat me, please,
With dignity,
And that's how I'll treat you.

We're gonna tell the teacher on you!
We're gonna tell the teacher on you!"

Wait a minute, wait a minute, that's no fair.
The teacher wasn't even there.
She won't know what it's about,
So let's sit down and work it out.

WHAT I WANT TO BE

The job I want is lots of fun.
And it's so special there's only one.

So whenever people ask me what I want to be,
I just tell them I want to be me.

BOBBY BROWN

Bobby Brown was feeling down.
His mommy and daddy were out of town.

He sat down and wrote them a letter.
Bobby Brown was feeling better.

REAL FRIENDS

Do you want to have some fun?"
  No, go away.
"Do you want to play and run?"
  No, not today.
"Do you want to be alone?"
  Yes, I do.
"I'll call you later on the phone."
  Hey — thank you.

THANKSGIVING DAY

We give thanks in late November.
But how about

January,
February,
March,
April,
May,
June,
July,
August,
September,
October,
And
December?

I think the best time for Thanksgiving
Is every day that we are living.

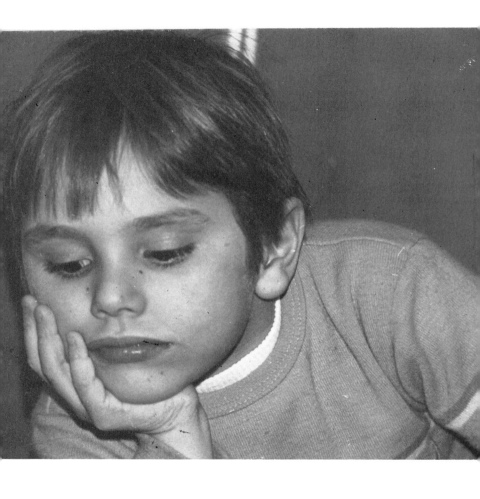

WHEN I'M BORED

When I'm bored
I just pretend
The world is coming to an end.

I think of things I didn't do
And I start doing
One or two.

MY BEST FRIEND

My best friend is very smart.
She always knows what's in my heart.
She may be busy, but every day
She stops and listens to what I say.

CHRISTMAS GIFT

What do you want for Christmas?
Ho, ho, ho!"

What do I want for Christmas?
I don't know.

I guess I want a ball
And a bat and a glove

And lots and lots and lots of
Love.

MISTAKES ARE GOOD

Mistakes are good,
They help us grow.
They show us what we need to know.

So when you make mistakes,
Don't cry.
You'll get better if you try.

I LOVE YOU

I love you" is hard to say,
Except in cards on Valentine's Day.
Maybe if we said it more
We could put an end to war.

IT'S GOOD FEELING BAD

It's good feeling bad.
Sometimes you should.
Then you appreciate
Feeling good.

AT LEAST I'M GETTING BETTER

I run and run and run and run
And then I trip and fall.
I throw and catch and throw and catch
And then I drop the ball.
I write my name a hundred times
And then I miss a letter.

But everybody makes mistakes...
At least I'm getting better!